ARROWS

OF

DELIVERANCE

"…Write the vision, and make it plain…"

Habakkuk 2:2   KJV

STACEY JAMES SARTIN

ARROWS OF DELIVERANCE

"…Write the vision, and make it plain

Habakkuk 2:2 KJV

Copyright © 2014 Stacey Sartin

ISBN1492845671

All Scripture quotations and references are taken from the King James version of the Bible.

Email: StaceySartin@me.com

DEDICATION

This book is dedicated to:

Reverend Sylvester Sartin, Jr.

Reverend Sylvester Sartin, Sr.

Reverend James Sartin

and

Elder Sartin, "the old preacher" that declared the Word of God in the cotton fields of Mississippi.

Through five generations, these men – my father, grandfather, great-grandfather and great-great-grandfather – have modeled the loving, meek and humble spirit of Christ. Their diligence, strength, character and spirit – as witnessed and received in the instruction handed down to me – are saving graces and eternal blessings from our Holy Father.

God bless you, Sirs!

To my wife and best friend, Kaneisha Sartin:

Thank you for believing in me.

I love you.

FOREWORD

My only son has done it again, lifting the creation of God for us to see how these things relate to our lives. Every time he preaches, he has the attention of the entire congregation.

Once I began to read Arrows of Deliverance, I couldn't put it down. Just as our Lord and Savior came to fulfill the Commandments of God, when you follow the steps in this book, your life will be enriched forever. You will never be the same. This book should be read by all of God's creation.

The way he interprets the sparrow, earthquakes, fire, rainbows, vessels, nets, trees, sheep, wolves and light with the Word of God is absolutely amazing.

Our Lord and Savior has blessed him to be a blessing to us.

Pastor Sylvester Sartin, Jr.

INTRODUCTION

God's love and His promises surround us. Everywhere you look, He speaks. Hearing and believing what He says is where we sometimes miss the mark. Our thrust for understanding and our zeal for performing His will is often off-target, until He points us in the right direction. It's through His Spirit, not our might or power, that we hit the bulls-eye in life.

His promises are like a bow; we are like the string. In His Word are our arrows of deliverance, thrusting our thoughts and actions toward the marks He has provided for peace, joy and prosperity in life. Those marks represent the higher calling He has for us in a relationship with Christ Jesus. Within that calling, all things work for our good.

As God draws us near, the operation is similar to how the bow and arrow works. God, as archer of our lives, pulls us out of our resting position and toward His face and ear. Like the string tied to the bow, we hold onto the promises of God but there is no power within us to release the promises. The unbent string represents our unbent will. As we lose our stubbornness and self-serving philosophies, we bend toward God and begin to communicate with Him through His Word. It's through His living Word, Jesus, that God hears us, and we hear Him.

His mercy allows us to bend but not break as He humbles us and draws us closer to His face. He will not stretch, bend or pull us beyond what we can bear. It is near His face that we see things from His vantage point. Here we have His ear and He has ours. At this point He hears clearly our cries for help and relief. We, in turn, hear His direction and purposes for our lives, before finally being released into His will.

While bending toward God, all of the promises He has made are also bending with us and towards us, building up power as the bow does when the string is pulled. As God releases us from humbling trials and experiences, His promises are released. As power is transferred from the bow to the arrow via the string, the power of God's Word and the fulfillment of His promises are transferred to us by the Spirit and released into our lives. We receive power to shoot down enemy situations and achieve desired goals.

Jesus is the Word of God, and the Word of God has all the arrows we need in life. Jesus knew no sin and did no wrong, therefore, He never "missed the mark."

Allowing God to guide your thoughts and actions will help you avoid missing the mark. My hope is that the Spirit-inspired words of this book "make straight the way" and allow you to hit the targets God has laid out in your life.

I love you.

God bless and keep you.

Reverend Stacey J. Sartin

CONTENTS

KEEP YOUR EYE ON THE SPARROW

Chapter One

"Look at the birds of the air; they neither sow nor reap nor gather into barns, and yet your heavenly Father feeds them. Are you not of more value than they?" Matthew 6:26

Sparrows are amazing birds. They're famous, too; made so by scripture references to God's care for them. God cares for sparrows. He provides for all their needs, leaving them free to enjoy existence. God cares for you. Are you free? Are you enjoying your existence, or do you just exist?

Follow a sparrow as he flies, and you'll notice grace – not within the sparrow but within God's eternal counsel as demonstrated by how the sparrow's flight is achieved. The sparrow is light in weight, which reduces the pull of gravity. Its bones are made of light-weight material but are still strong enough to maintain a core. In a fruitful Christian life, you must also be light in weight, setting aside those sins that can so easily overtake us. These sins are weight because they allow the devil – our spiritual gravity – to pull us down.

The sparrow is covered in feathers that allow rain to roll off and wind to blow over and through them easily. The children of God are covered by messages of hope in Christ. The scriptural references to God's power, purpose and will for our lives buffet the rain in our lives. The winds of sorrow and misfortune blow by as we use God's Word for direction and comfort, and as we rest under Christ's rule in our hearts.

The sparrow also has three bones connected together in its back that are strong enough to tolerate the power needed to begin flight. This bone is called the furcula, but it is best known as the wishbone. The wishbone strengthens the skeletal structure in birds to help withstand the dramatic rigors of flying. Without these three fused bones, flight would be impossible, and the sparrow would break its back during takeoff. In our Christian life, those three bones are represented by the Father, Son, and Holy Spirit. We need them behind us if we are ever to take off in life. Without them, flight is impossible. Hence, you see many spiritually crippled Christians, who attempt to fly and end up unable to even maintain a walk with Christ.

The sparrow uses the principle of thrust and lift to begin flight. The thrust pertains to how the sparrow throws itself
upward into open space. The thrust represents the faith of the Christian. We must throw ourselves upward into the open space of God even when we don't see what will hold us there. Sometimes those spaces seem to be empty and unable to sustain the wishes and desires that we possess. Faith allows us to thrust ourselves into His will anyway.

KEEP YOUR EYES ON THE SPARROW

For the sparrow, the lift occurs after the thrust. The light weight of the sparrow and the power of his thrust allow for air to flow under and over its wings, creating a lift if the wings are open. For people, elevation in life occurs when we believe God, trust God and put our faith in Him. When we stop allowing a life of sin and guilt to ground us, combined with a Christian walk that creates opportunities instead of denying them, the power of God lifts us to new heights. Ideas we thought would never work come to fruition. We're able to fill empty spaces in our lives and soar to achievements we only imagined we could ever reach.

However, the sparrow's powerful and consistent wing flapping demands a considerable amount of energy. In addition to a force called drag, which constantly pushes against the sparrow as it flies, the sparrow is also battling the ever-present pull of gravity, winds, inclement weather, natural predators, and a host of other draining challenges of flight. But the sparrow is armed. It is blessed with a metabolism that generates the energy needed to battle antagonists and to continue flight without easily tiring.

In our lives in Christ, we also would tire quickly in our battle against the evil forces in our lives. These forces appear to press against each move toward a good opportunity. These forces pull us down, rain on our parade, prey upon us, and attempt to weaken our faith in God and our belief in His promises. But like the sparrow, we are blessed and equally armed.

A Christian's spiritual metabolism is extremely high which makes us hungry for the word of God. We are constantly seeking and eating the word which builds our faith and increases our belief system. Thereby are we able to resist the devil and withstand his constant attacks.

As the sparrow continues to climb upward and gain momentum, a rhythm develops and various wing movements create different flight patterns such as soaring and diving. Flight becomes easier and altitude increases, allowing for greater distances to be traveled. The sparrow's opportunities to see food and shelter also increase. It is able also to spot enemies and avoid dangerous places. So goes our flight in the Spirit. As we grow in God's Word our routine changes. Some places we frequented, we no longer go. Some hands we held, we now only shake. Our highs are higher, and lows no longer seem and feel as low. Praising God and sharing our faith with others becomes easier and is done with newfound confidence. God takes us places we could not reach, and we see things in new light, uncovering things once hidden in the darker parts of our lives. The wisdom God provides us identifies enemies and rough spots as it leads us along prosperous pathways.

Even as sparrows must stop flight to rest, so must we. Observe the sparrow in rest. The simplest illustration of God's care of the sparrow is when it's resting on a telephone wire.

Have you ever seen a sparrow perched and at rest on a wire? It just sits there, looking side-to-side with a gentle spirit of smugness, quickly bobbing its head in all directions, and then, just sitting there. It's as if it doesn't have a care in the universe; no enemies can get to it. It can see food sources and other necessities that may be near. It can practice its whistle and congregate with the flock.

Even if the wind is blowing and the wire begins the swing, the sparrow doesn't move. Cats and dogs may come by and look up menacingly, but the sparrow seems to barely notice. Nothing seems to move it. Why? How?

On the back of its legs, the sparrow has flexor tendons that allow the legs to bend and straighten. The flexor tendons cause the sparrow's feet to curl and lock into position whenever it bends its knees. As long as the knees are bent, the feet remain locked. When it lands on a wire, it bends its knees to lock its feet around the wire. Nothing can prevail against this rest unless the sparrow unbends its knees.

In our lives, when we seek rest and peace within God's purpose and will for our lives and when we bend our knees in prayer, we lock ourselves into communion with God. In this place, on this wire, in His will, we are free from the cares of the world. We become open to God's healing mercies and grace. The enemy can't reach us. We see clearly what God has provided for our prosperity and well-being. Nothing can prevail against us and no weapon formed against us can prosper.

The next time you are near a wire, look up, and keep your eye on the sparrow. God is taking good care of it, so you know He is taking good care of you!

MAKE YOUR EARTH QUAKE

Chapter Two

"And, behold, there was a great earthquake: for the angel of the Lord descended from heaven, and came and rolled back the stone from the door, and sat upon it." Matthew 28:2

Matthew 15:1-5 says: "In the end of the Sabbath, as it began to dawn toward the first day of the week, came Mary Magdalene and the other Mary to see the sepulchre. And, behold, there was a great earthquake: for the angel of the Lord descended from heaven, and came and rolled back the stone from the door, and sat upon it. His countenance was like lightning, and his raiment white as snow: And for fear of him the keepers did shake, and became as dead men. And the angel answered and said unto the women, Fear not ye for

I know that ye seek Jesus, which was crucified."

The preceding verses show the disciples of Jesus going to His grave to anoint His body for burial on the third day after His crucifixion. Have you really considered how terribly distraught they must have been? Jesus was their *HOPE*; they had placed all they had in Him. He was their present and their future, but now, He was dead.

With His body in that borrowed cave, covered with stone and guarded by enemy soldiers, lay the hope that had changed the diciples' lives. Tradition called for His body to be anointed and they were following ceremony. Ceremony suddenly had replaced hope.

When we lose hope, a foundation in Christ, a steady diet of Bible-reading, church attendance, spiritual music and most importantly, daily prayer will keep us moving in the direction of God's deliverance. It's when we change our routine and give up because we believe all hope is lost that we have the hardest time getting things back on track. We need to establish and keep a routine in Christ.

This is pain Jesus' disciples carried in each step they took that early morning as they approached His grave. The same pain we feel today when our hope is lost and buried in an inaccessible grave. It is a dark hour with no hint of daylight and the only steps to take are within whatever path we have worn in life. A death, a loss of something or someone valuable and instrumental to our happiness and well being; a physical impairment or shortcoming; a disappointment in our expectations of ourselves or others.

But God had a message for them in their faithfulness. It's well known that it is darkest before the dawn but we have to continue to seek God's wisdom and comfort, even in the worst of times. The midnight hour must hold the same perseverance as the noon hour. *Hope* was not lost but had risen from the grave they were seeking.

Hope lies where you put it, and when it is gone, routine is the safety net. Going back to what you know to do is natural and profitable if you know Christ. An excellent example is found in the familiar release doves used at weddings and funerals.

These homing pigeons are known to travel more than 1,100 miles during migration and return to the same nest to mate every year. Many believe the birds use the small amounts of iron found in their beaks to read the Earth's south and north magnetic poles, guiding themselves with a built-in compass. Some believe the birds use memorials and monuments, like barns, highways, rivers or mountains as guideposts and landmarks on the trip. There are as many ideas existing as to why and how birds do this as there are suggestions about how *we* can find our way in life.

In our Christian journey, we, too, have "magnetite," but we call it the Holy Spirit. It guides us to and fro, leading us into remembrance of all that Christ taught. When we develop a "migration path" or routine in God, we create "landmarks and monuments" and habits that keep you in line with God's plan until we can see our way. As we give testimony and witness to God's work and goodness in our lives, we remember the lessons learned and deliverances gained. This allows us to keep moving in our darkest hour, the hours just before dawn.

Angels are messengers of God. The angel these women met at the grave gave a message that caused the Earth to quake. When the earth quaked, the stone hiding hope was removed, and the disciples were able to regain what they had lost.

Our lives are altered when we receive God's life-altering Word and the obstacles to hope in our lives are removed. At that point, our earth is quaked. At the crust, the earth is made up of seven plates that fit together like loose, slow moving puzzle pieces. The edge of each puzzle piece is a major fault line. The sides of the fault lines move smoothly past each other if there are no points protruding and causing conflict with the adjacent plates. The fault lines become stress points when conflict is introduced. Friction builds as they shift, move and scrape against one another. When the friction builds up

enough energy, the heat strong enough to melt and liquefy rocks and dirt is released upward from the earth's crust. When this energy reaches the surface, it radiates outward in waves and the ground is displaced and shakes imitating the ripples of a rock thrown in still waters. This is what we call a natural earthquake.

Just like the Earth, our daily lives are made up of pieces that often puzzle us. We, too, have faults in our lives. Sometimes, the puzzling pieces in our lives are able to move past one another with ease and cause no stress. These faults or sins in our lives often cause stress. These shortcomings are why we are able to appear as God-fearing saints one hour and prove ourselves sinful devils the next. When we ignore God's Word, we lose focus of the messages that provide the energy and opportunity to better ourselves and enrich our lives. Without the Word of God truly directing our lives, it becomes easy to separate identities and maintain opposite purposes in different areas of our lives.

Friends at school or work may know a completely different person than do our fellow choir members. Our wives and husbands may have no idea who we are with friends and acquaintances. However, if we develop a routine that adds value to our life, things will change. God's message of hope and salvation through Jesus Christ will cause a conflict within our faults and cause our Earth to quake.

The energy from the epicenter of an earthquake is so powerful that it creates temperatures that melt the solid rock and earth above it. That is why the earth moves and rolls like waves of water during an earthquake – the ground has become soft and pliable. When we receive and act upon God's Word, the spiritual energy and power therein will heat up the foundation of our lives and break up the hard things covering the faults within us. This energy will start within and come to the surface in our life. The way we act, the things we do and say will change. Things that were not sturdy or shaky will be toppled. Things that were lifted up to high for proper balance in life will be brought lower. Things that are stable and grounded in truth and righteousness will continue to stand, being proven and strengthened in position.

Depending on the earthquake type, different landscape changes result. Some quakes cause plates to overlap another as they collide. This is how mountain ranges are formed. These quakes happen in our lives when God wants to elevate us in an area of life and lower our focus and dependence on another area. This is how our highest achievements are attained. This is how we reach our mountain tops.

Some quakes cause two plates that were close to separate. God creates rifts and distance between us and things or people we hold dear. Other quakes create islands in the middle of nowhere by creating mountains in the sea, just as God brings new people and situations into our lives seemingly out of nowhere.

The enemy guards were frozen in fear and unable to move while the disciples went easily around them to receive the message and view the evidence. Our enemies are also stilled as we receive and accept God's message of salvation and *hope*. We are able to do things in Christ that the enemies and obstacles in life had blocked. We are now able to go around them to see better and achieve more.

Aftershocks are earthquakes that occur after the initial earthquake as the fault line adjusts to the main shock. Aftershocks are in the same region but smaller than the main shock. In our lives we can create aftershocks in God's message of hope by praying, reading and meditating on His Word.

The epicenter of an earthquake is the spot directly over where the earthquake started, however, earthquakes have a ripple effect that cause the same energy to be felt in areas near the earthquake. When our life settles for the better after our earth quakes, we affect our family, neighbors, friends, coworkers and schoolmates. The relationships change and the message of hope is spread. Focusing on God's messages, will make your earth quake. When it does, especially at the point of our shortcomings, our world will change for the better.

Make your earth quake!

TRIAL BY FIRE

Chapter Three

"Then Nebuchadnezzar the king was astonied. And he rose up in haste and spake and said to his counsellors, Did not we cast three men bound into the midst of the fire?...And the princes, governors, and captains, and the king's counsellors, being gathered together, saw these men, upon whose bodies the fire had no power, nor was an hair of their head singed, neither were their coats changed, nor the smell of fire had passed on them."

Daniel 3:24-27

The young Hebrew princes in Daniel had no chance in the fiery furnace they had been thrown into, just as we appear to have no chance when we get into heated situations. However, this fiery trial would prove to be a test and testimony of faith, hope and patience for all generations. To examine the odds these men faced, look at how fire burns wood. Fire is the visible side effect of something changing form; it comes from a chemical reaction between oxygen and a fuel source, which is wood in our example. When wood is heated by fire to 300 degrees the cellulose, the material of which wood is made, starts to decompose. Some of the materials that decompose are released into the air, which is what we see as smoke. Smoke is made up of oxygen, carbon and hydrogen.

At about 500 degrees, the compounds in wood start to break up and recombine to make other compounds. As the compounds break up and recombine with other molecules, their light weight causes them to rise so fast they create light. We see the light in the form of flames.

In our lives, when things get hot – mentally stressful and spiritually troubling – we tend to change our thinking and begin to consider alternatives to present actions and circumstances. When God's Spirit moves in our lives and heats things up, a spiritual reaction occurs. We begin to let go of things that we learn are unnecessary or detrimental. The fiery trials discard the dross we don't deed. The unfit and ineffective things we had mixed in with our daily routines are replaced with self-improvements. As we change, those around us recognize this as our "light shining." We are even said to be on fire for Christ.

Another side effect of the rapid decomposing and recombining of molecules is a lot of heat. This same heat in our lives changes the composition of the people and the things around us. Conversations evolve around elevated subjects as our flames for Christ shoot upward. Relationships are formed around new interests and habits as we let go of the unrefined things in life and grab hold to a better way.

What's even more comforting is that fire is self-perpetuating. The heat of flames itself keeps the wood at the right temperature to start burning and continue burning as long as there is oxygen and wood. In the same fashion, our flames continue to burn as long as we have the Spirit and faith in the Word of God. Our own light provides self-encouragement to continue our walk with God. Seeing victory after victory and mercy after grace encourages

us to remain faithful and steadfast.

The size of the wood also determines how easily it will catch fire. It takes longer for a thick tree to catch fire than a toothpick because there is less to heat up. In our lives, it takes us longer to warm up to the things of God when the cares of the world weigh us down. The fewer worries and worldly concerns we carry, the easier it is to depend on and glorify God.

Daniel had confidence when he walked within the fiery furnace. Knowing that the God he served would use weapons seemingly formed against him to glorify Himself. Knowing that he would come through this trial whole.

We, too, can have this same confidence. We can rest assured that the fiery trials of life will not even singe our clothes if we allow God to walk, talk and guide us through them. With this confidence we can "glory in our tribulations" as the early Christians did because all problems become opportunities to experience victory in Christ. Even when the Word of God and His comfort seem distant and limited, our faith and passion for Christ can be reignited in the same way backdrafts restart flames.

A backdraft occurs as a fire is dies out, and oxygen is reintroduced to the area. An explosion occurs and the fire reignites. When our spiritual zeal has decreased and we feel like our strength in Christ is waning, we can reignite our fires through increasing our time in God's presence. We can read more Scripture for wisdom. We can pray and meditate to learn God's purpose and will in our circumstances. All it takes is one spark to ignite a backdraft, and all it takes is one Word from God to ignite us spiritually. We can assemble ourselves with other believers who have experience with our obstacles and glean direction. We can blow off and blow up our dying nature by correcting wrong steps and redirecting our paths.

However, not all fires in our lives are tests to prove God's glory through our faith. Some trials are created by sin and are the honest wages or our disobedience. Even these trials can be overcome through Christ. They can be put out through the Word in the same manner that firefighters put out flames.

Firefighters don't point their water at the smoke and soot; they aim for the source of the flame. In our lives, we must read the Word in search of ways to apply it to our everyday circumstances. The wisdom we receive from God is given to help us overcome obstacles and live life more abundantly.

Firefighters also wave the water back and forth to ensure all sources of the flame are smothered. We, too, should apply God's wisdom to all areas of our lives, ensuring that all parts of our existence are covered by God's grace and mercy – our family, our jobs, our friends, school, everything.

Just as firefighters have been provided with the appropriate tools to do their job, Christians have been given a similar advantage. When an auto accident occurs and a person is trapped inside mangled and twisted steel, the Jaws of Life are brought out. This tool allows firefighters to pry open metal to rescue victims. When the situations that move us through life collide with unforeseen circumstances, Christians use our spiritual jaws of life – the Word of mouth – to pry our trapped souls from wrecked lives.

Sometimes, fire depletes the oxygen in an environment to the point firefighters need oxygen masks. Our oxygen is the spirit of God, and the Bible is the oxygen mask we use to continue working in Spirit-less environments with God-less people. In the same manner firefighters must extend ladders to reach victims at higher floors, we must extend our selves beyond our comfort zones to share the good news we have with people beyond our everyday reach.

Fire-resistant gear must be worn during rescue activities. Hate, apathy, strife, envy – these things accelerate fires. Peace, love, gentleness, kindness – these things are fire-resistant. Appropriate armor is necessary to save others and prevent getting burned yourself. Put on the whole armor of God, which includes a vest that will quench the fiery darts of the devil. That armor is made whole by covering all aspects of your life with the wisdom and direction provided by the Word of God.

SEEING THE RAINBOW

Chapter Four

"I do set my bow in the cloud, and it shall be for a token of a covenant between me and the earth. And it shall come to pass, when I bring a cloud over the earth, that the bow shall be seen in the cloud: And I will remember my covenant, which is between me and you and every living creature of all flesh: and the waters shall no more become a flood to destroy all flesh. And the bow shall be in the cloud; and I will look upon it, that I may remember the everlasting covenant between God and every living creature of all flesh that is upon the earth." Genesis 9:13-16

19

Water accumulates and rises in the air around us. It gathers above and becomes clouds. When too much water has gathered, it becomes too heavy to float and begins to drop back down to Earth as droplets we call rain.

In our lives, situations, responsibilities, activities and outcomes build up daily. The challenges of life keep coming, and they don't slow down. When they begin to block wise decisions and prudent paths, difficulties arise and problems rain down.

Many see rain as punishment, however, rain is a gift from God, sent to cleanse our environments and enlighten our minds to the promises He has made to us in His Word.

Rain is as plentiful as his Word, and God has created a natural and spiritual system that keeps us in steady supply of this blessing.

The water cycle is a term used to describe the continuous movement of water beneath the earth, on the earth, to the sky and from the sky. It's like a Ferris wheel taking water up and bringing water down in different forms.

The sun initiates the water cycle. In one form of the cycle, the sun heats up water in oceans, lakes and rivers. The warmed water evaporates into small floating drops of water called water vapor. Wind blows the water vapor around the world, it collides and collects with other water vapor, and eventually becomes the aforementioned heavy clouds and releases the water back to earth as rain to repeat the cycle.

Much more of the water in the world is held in the oceans, lakes, rivers, and underwater reservoirs than there is water moved back and forth within the water cycle. In our lives, there is more power within us through the Word of God than we can imagine. It's a small thing to overcome anything the world rains on you if you learn and trust the solutions that Christ has provided. His Word is an umbrella for those rainy days. You don't have to stay indoors and put off responsibilities, goals and accomplishments. With God, you can achieve these things in the sun, in the rain, in the noon day and in the midnight hour. Wherever you stand in hope in Him, there He is giving power and strength congruent to your faith.

The believer's prayer cycle works the same way as the water cycle. The prayer cycle is a continuous movement of God's Word from the believer on Earth to God in heaven and from God in Heaven to the believer on earth. The Word we receive from God is returned to Him in various forms such as prayer, hymns, songs, goodwill toward others, benevolent acts, testimony and thanks to God for His benefits.

God tells us in His Word what to expect in life and how to deal with these expectations. When we face situations that His Word addresses, we pray for His Word to manifest its truth and power over that situation and we act according to the direction the Word gives us. The 100%-success rate of this cycle is its benefit to us and a testimony to the power of God and His faithfulness. He proves time and time again that He will do what He says He will do.

So, as we see the natural water cycle raining problems down on us, we have hope and power to overcome these issues through Christ. We know we have a spiritual prayer cycle that rains down solutions to every problem we face. We're sure we have a direct line to God who will listen to us as we remind Him of His promises in which we have come to believe and trust.

As we exercise this confidence, our stature in spirit grows, and our mind and vision are elevated. When one looks up on a clear day, one sees the sun. When Christians look up in life, we see the Son. Likewise, when one looks up on a rainy day, one sees rain, but when Christians look up on a day raining with trouble, we see a *rainbow*.

Rainbows are caused by the reflection of sunlight in raindrops. The different colors of the rainbow appear because the white light we see as daylight is broken down to reveal some of the many colors of which it is really made. The breakdown, called refraction, occurs when the light enters the raindrop and again after it reflects off back of the raindrop. There are more colors in a rainbow than the seven colors we see with the naked eye (red, orange, yellow, green, blue, indigo and violet); however, the other colors move at a wavelength our eyes and brain cannot receive and interpret. Three conditions must exist for us to see a rainbow:

1. The sun must be behind us.
2. Rain or suspended water droplets.
3. You must be looking up at a 40- to 42-degree angle.

In our lives, the promises of God only can be seen through the Son. Often, we find ourselves turned away from Jesus or not focused on Him completely. We find ourselves with our backs to Him. These are the days we see rain in our lives. However, even though we can't see Him, He has promised to be with us always. He has promised to take care of us in times of trouble and need.

So, when it's raining in our lives we are still able to look up. We maintain hope, and our attitudes remain cheerful, kind and expectant. We avoid depressed thoughts and wayward activities that obscure the view of the promises we see in Christ.

By keeping our focus on Jesus during troubles, we use the counsel and wisdom of His teachings to overcome. He sees our faith and sends help through new ideas, solutions, helpful believers lifting us in love and support. His Word promises all these things and, as we read and believe Scripture, these promises become clearer in the face of trials and tribulations.

When it rains, we suffer and are reminded of how Jesus suffered unto death on the cross. The promises of God are demonstrated in the rainbow that follows the rain in our lives. We see the red, innocent blood being spilled to pay for our crimes and free us from guilt and sin. We see the orange tint of a rising Sun after a dark hour. We see the green pastures in life to which He has promised to lead us. We see His glorious and triumphant return with the saints in blue skies in the last day, and we see indigo as all things are put under His power and eternal, purple majesty is transitioned from all things to our conquering King. We begin to see life in more detail and realize that life's biggest problems and concerns can be broken down into solvable issues if we use the wisdom and confidence found in a Christian life. Once dreaded trials become celebrated opportunities to improve our lives and glorify God through a personal demonstration of His power.

No one sees the same rainbow because rainbows are not in an exact physical location. The rainbow you see is reflecting off the raindrops in front of you at the angle from which you're looking. The person standing in the rain next to you sees a different rainbow in a different space, if they see it at all. So just as your problems belong to you, the promises God has for you are for you. Every relationship with God is personal.

You have to look up and see His promises for yourself. You have to make sure the Son is in your life. If you don't see the promises, He is not there. If His Spirit is not reminding you of His Words, He is not there. If you are not inclined to look to God for all your help, He is not there.

Not all of the colors of light are visible to us. Not all of God's purposes in our lives will be explained and revealed in our time. We see things darkly now, but one day, all things will be made visible for us to know the breadth and depth of God's glory. For now, the Word helps to reveal the things we need to know and provides us with faith, patience and hope to wait on God as we go through things we don't understand. You have to face your troubles knowing that the power and light of God is behind you. You have to know that when you believe and trust God, He will reveal all the solutions you need to overcome any challenge you face. You have to see the *rainbow*, and then, you'll see His promises.

VESSELS

Chapter Five

"What if God, willing to shew his wrath, and to make his power known, endured with much longsuffering the vessels of wrath fitted to destruction: And that he might make known the riches of his glory on the vessels of mercy, which he had afore prepared unto glory..."
Romans 9:22-23

By primary definition in English, a vessel is a container for holding something. Vessels are an able example of our lives before God, our Creator. In much the same way a potter crafts a vessel made of clay, wood and porcelain; our God crafts us as containers for the spiritual and natural resources that manifest His will. Clay is a natural material composed of fine-grained minerals formed from the weathering and erosion of rocks. Clay is soft and pliable but hardens when dried or heated at high temperatures. That's why it's used in pottery. When a potter begins a work of clay, it is thrown onto the center of a potter's wheel as a lump of clay. When God begins His life changing work in us, we are spiritually shapeless. No form of Godliness is demonstrated consistently in our lives, but God "centers" us within His plan. He surrounds us with His Word and directs our paths. We're no longer on the outside looking in at the hope found in Christ. Our thoughts, our activities and our desires start to center on God-given principles and instruction.

The potter controls the speed of the turning wheel with the step of His foot just as God controls the times and seasons in our lives. We must walk with Him at His pace and within His appointed times. Just as the potter stops the wheel to focus on a particular area or to correct a faulted side, God brings about times when we must have patience as His power moves in certain areas and weak points for us.

The potter keeps the wheel and clay moist so that it is pliable and can stretch, pull and fold into the desired shape and size for a particular vessel's intended load. God uses His Word to change our hardened hearts – that hold their position in the face of any offenses or shortcomings of others – to softened hearts, flexible enough to bend toward kindness, love, forgiveness, and the other fruits from the Tree of Life.

Once the potter is ready to begin creating the cavity of the vessel, he holds a thumb up and then turns it down. We once had a thumbs-up relationship with God through Adam, but disobedience turned it thumbs-down. However, through Christ, God is working on us and creating a new inside that will glorify Him on the outside. Once the soft clay is opened and molded into a hollow shape, walls are added. Without walls, anything poured into it would fall out. In our lives, we often mistake the gift of knowing that God is real with having Him living inside of us. Just confessing God exists does not bring salvation. Jesus says come to Him. Lay down your burdens and take up His. Put the cares in life that are weighing you down to second place in life, and put Jesus first. The first load will give you strength to carry the second. The burdens He gives you are light to carry and the things He wants to tell you are easy to follow. The paths worldly wisdom provides become burdens within themselves and you end up pulling these issues through life in an uphill battle with no victory in sight.

The potter forms the walls by gently pulling them upward as he spins the wheel. He is careful not to pull too hard or quickly, knowing that even a small tear could force him to restart the project from the beginning. Still, the potter often restarts because the clay is unbalanced or too dry. When we seek God, He elevates our spirits and minds in Him. He changes our surroundings by lifting them to a higher state of purpose and direction. Areas of life where we were unable to hold enough energy and wisdom to be successful are now our strengths. Ideals and goals we were unable to attain are now ours or within reach. Lessons learned are not easily forgotten. Scriptures and Godly wisdom is readily recalled when needed. Solutions are found, as long as we continue reading the Word, praying daily and fellowshipping with God and other believers. This is the process God uses to "raise our walls."

A process called flooring occurs next. In this step the potter flattens and rounds the bottom of the pot. In our walk with God, this is the step where God humbles us and lowers our dependence on our own inner resources. He shapes our hearts and minds into believers that follow His way. Trimming also occurs about this time. This is where the potter removes excess clay from the vessel, mirroring God's removal of our bondage to our sinful nature as He separates us from our past desires and practices to sanctify us. Firing is the final and most important step in the potter's creative process. Like clay, believers are formed by the gradual weathering and

erosion of sin and worldly influence. God allows difficulties in life to break down believers so that He can reshape hearts and minds according to His will. Believers are baptized in the Holy Spirit of God, thereby initiating our firing process. This is when our life in Christ really starts to heat up.

The firing process changes the molecular makeup of pottery and it cannot be reversed. In God's firing process, He allows us to face situations and challenges that prove and test our faith. These tests take us through circumstances that force inner and outer changes if we are to overcome them. Our spiritual makeup is altered in ways that cannot be reversed. Once we are truly believers, nothing can separate us from the love of God.

The three major types of pottery further illustrate God's work in our lives: earthenware, stoneware and porcelain. Earthenware is the oldest form of clay pottery. This type of pottery was fired in pits or open bonfires and made without decoration. The relatively low firing temperature leaves earthenware porous and a bad choice for liquids, which would easily leak out. It also is easily chipped and cracked, but its low cost and simple work process make it a favorite choice of some potters.

Worldly believers are most similar to earthenware. They don't study or regularly read God's word. Prayer time is rare and quick, and they have distaste for going through any tests or proving their faith in God.

Theses earthen believers take the easy road and follow the path of least resistance, especially when led by sin and destructive suggestions. They rarely attend religious services with fellow believers and spend little time sharing Christ with others. These vessels are easily provoked, saddened and discouraged and are unable to show love to others because they have little to carry and not enough to pour out. Any Word from God or encouragement from true believers "leaks" out and is ignored or quickly forgotten in time of trouble. However, many believers are satisfied with this type of walk because of the low requirements, despite the fact that it does not produce much fruit. Stoneware is fired at a higher temperature than earthenware. Stoneware also

is glazed, eliminating the remaining porous tendencies. Glazing is a technique whereby a glassy coating is added to the vessel before firing. The primary purpose of glazing is decoration and protection. In the same vein, stoneware believers are willing and prepared to examine themselves within the trials they face in life. Godly wisdom, spiritual lessons and holy guidance are sought and followed with reverence. These believers surround themselves in pastoral leadership, Christian fellowship, biblical instruction and a strong prayer life. This consolidated spiritual coating keeps worldly influences at bay and prevents the loss of spiritual insight gained.

The strongest pottery is porcelain. Porcelain is fired at a high enough temperature to prevent any loss of liquid. It is firm and its molecules vibrate relative to the frequencies in the air around it making it less likely to shatter or crack from environmental feedback. The strength, transparency and whiteness of porcelain are derived from the transformation of the clay into glass and tough minerals during the high-temperature firing process.

Porcelain models believers who have gone through the fires of life putting all their trust in God. They have allowed the Spirit of God to shape their lives and guide their walk. They believe God and are able to achieve all the purposes that God has for them because they have seen what God can do in seemingly impossible situations.

They do not hide from God; instead they confess their sins. Like porcelain china, by the sacrifice and blood of Christ, they are made white as snow. God's Word declares there is no condemnation of self or others in them. They are able to withstand the valleys and humble themselves at the heights because they hold the promises of God within – none leak out or are forgotten. They seek to model the integrity and character of Christ; making every attempt able to pour the love of God upon others at the command of the Spirit. The firing process of God makes these vessels more than decorative items, but vessels of mercy from God unto man.

Examine yourself and name the vessel reflecting your spirit. Earthenware?

Stoneware? Porcelain? Know what you hold and what you pour out. Be sure you are allowing the firing process to mold and strengthen you into a "vessel of mercy…prepared unto glory."

ON FIRE FOR GOD

Chapter Six

"Then I said, I will not make mention of him, nor speak any more in his name. But his word was in mine heart as a burning fire shut up in my bones…" Jeremiah 20:9

The ability to control fire is a major achievement of man, to say the least. Fire is essential to man's everyday survival and comfort. It is used to generate heat and warmth when faced with cold and inclement environments. Fire is used to cook foods. It is used to deter predators and ward off intruders. Perhaps, most importantly, fire is used to create light. Jesus commanded us to be lights to the world. He ignited a flame in us to generate and sustain the warmth He brought to the cold and hostile environments we face. Jesus directed us to provide a good flavor to the world's diet, just as salt seasons meat, thereby adding the consideration of brotherly love and Godly living to the choices men have before them. We are told to warn others of false advisors and half-truths, to edify one another other and protect from each other from evil people and circumstances. Jesus wants us to be on fire for Him.

Fire begins with a chemical process called combustion. When a flammable or combustible material is subjected to enough heat and is able to sustain a chain reaction, a flame ignites. Acknowledging Jesus as the Son of God and accepting salvation through belief in His life, death and resurrection for our sins is a *spiritual* combustion process. When we take on this belief system, demonstrated usually by looping together church assembly, daily prayer, bible study, meditation on God and other believing behaviors, we are ignited in Christ and become lights that reveal Him to others.

The flame we see in fire is a mix of gases and solids reacting to the heat of the combustion process. The chemical bonds that exist in the burning material break up, rise and form new bonds and compounds. Likewise, the flame we see in believers is a mix of our beliefs and actions reacting to our faith in Christ and our walk in the Spirit. As our lives heat up in Jesus, the connections we had with people and places outside of God's plans for lives break off. We begin seeking higher pursuits and forming new relationships and goals in life.

The heat-accelerated rise of the lightened gases and solids in the combustion process is what creates the light of the flame. The freed materials move upwards so fast that we see them as light. In the same manner, our sudden move from wrongs to rights, from bad to good creates a spiritual light against the dark background of our past lives. The new attitudes and behaviors in believers attract the attention of those surrounding us.

Every flame behaves differently, depending on its surroundings. So it is with people that follow the teachings of Christ. God has a plan for each of us and supplies us with the resources to follow His plan. Just as flames dance in reaching for new bonds that happen to be nearby, our lights shine for those who God has determined it will shine upon. He supplies us with what is needed to attract and sustain the spiritual attention of others, be it forgiveness, a listening ear, a kind or helpful word, financial support or other actions favored by God.

Complete combustion occurs when all the gases and solids in a material are burned to their respective melting points. In the real world, this does not occur because there are always solids or gases within the burning material that have a melting point beyond the temperature of the flame. Even though we "walk in the Spirit" and are not "of the world," we are in the world. Being such, we have flaws and imperfections that will keep us short of meeting all our spiritual goals and obligations. The incombustible materials in flames are released as soot and smoke. The incombustible materials in the thoughts and actions of believers are the sins that have been forgiven through the atoning death of Jesus on the cross.

Jesus was the true light and, hence, the igniting flame that demonstrated the character of God. Though He was eternal, His brightest work was performed when He descended from heaven and demonstrated love on Earth as a man. Jesus' Commandment to His followers was to love one another. We are to give each other ground support.

Forest fire colors are different at different levels because fire is hottest near the ground. There is more material to burn there: leaves, grass, shrubs. In a fire, a spectrum of colors exists that go from blue to red. The fire gets cooler and materials less combustible as the material changes to a less dense and less flammable fuel source. Each level of colors has more incombustible compounds than the last, until finally the aforementioned smoke is released at the red level – where no combustion takes place. The fire loses its impact.

We have varying gifts and impacts on different people and places, depending on where we are in our spiritual lives but the greatest gift is love. When operating in love, we have the brightest light and make strongest impact. If we move from this primary source of spiritual power, we lose power to affect our environment and eventually taper off and die out like flames that have burned out their fuel.

Our brightest moments in Christ involve showing sincere love for one another in speech and deed. Our primary function as believers is to love one another. Actions and thoughts that are not in line with this plan cause us to struggle. As these impurities are burned away in life, we are left with a pure flame that reaches to heaven providing what the ancient writers described as a "sweet savor" in God's nostrils.

God uses us to landscape our environment through "controlled burns." One method of extinguishing a fire is to remove its fuel source. Smaller fires are set in front of raging main fires to burn up all of the grass, shrubs and trees ahead. When the main fire gets to that point of forest, it goes out because it has nothing to keep it going. God has given those who follow Christ wisdom to discern good from evil. The spiritual insight therein allows believers to see people, places and circumstances as they present themselves and where they will lead. Believers use this light to avoid choices or lifestyles that can lead to ruin or stagnation. That same light is what believers shine on unbelievers when giving Godly advice.

Sometimes when a large volume of gas is burned, the sudden release of excessive air pressure is accompanied by a large noise we know as an explosion. When an unbeliever begins to believe and undergoes the combustion process ignited by the Holy Spirit, the release of long-suffered guilt, painful memories and hopelessness can generate a spiritual explosion. This explains a great deal of the initial excitement and readiness in new believers to "do everything" for Christ. Sustaining the flame is best achieved by an unfeigned love of God in prayer and meditation and by practicing loving acts of kindness and generosity as directed by the Spirit. Much consideration must also be given to conflagration, which is an intense, uncontrolled, destructive blaze. God wants us to follow the paths in which he leads us. God's fires are controlled and follow paths with certain road markers such as peace, love, joy, forgive and patience with others – that ensure we stay on the course. Again, we are the "salt of the earth" and should be enhancing human life by exampling the abundant life Jesus has given us. Controlled blazes enhance life. Uncontrolled blazes threaten life.

A conflagration can be accidental, natural or intentional. This is why Jesus told His followers to examine themselves. A believer should be wary of misunderstanding or misapplying the word of God and Christian doctrine. Unbelievers could be falsely led astray and end up in worse positions than they started. A believer should be careful of becoming familiar with ungodly people, places and activities. Like wildfire, these natural events ignite and spread quickly. A believer should also recognize God's voice and plan. A sincere relationship with God accompanied by true spiritual worship is the key to walking with God and knowing when He is directing us.

The good news is that once your fire starts, it will never go out. Fire, like a relationship with Jesus is self-perpetuating. The heat of the flame keeps the burning material at the temperature it took to start the fire. The fire burns as long as there is oxygen and fuel around it. If your heart is ablaze for God, Jesus is your fire, the Word of God is your oxygen and you are the fuel around Him. Your flame is eternal. Let your light shine. Be on fire for God!

LET DOWN YOUR NETS

Chapter Seven

"…he said to Simon, "Launch out into the deep and let down your nets for a draught." And Simon answering said unto him, "Master, we have toiled all night and have taken nothing; nevertheless at thy word I will let down the net." And when they had done this, they inclosed a great number of fishes: and their net brake. And they beckoned unto their partners which were in the other ship, that they should come and help them. And they came, and filled both the ships…" Luke 5:4-7

Jesus often challenges us to succeed at opportunities appearing destined for failure. He demonstrated this when he asked some of his followers to return to fishing after unsuccessfully trolling all night. Trusting him, albeit with some hesitation, they returned to fishing and pulled in a haul so large it almost toppled their boat. Those same challenges exist for us today in the oft ignored opportunities that greet us in everyday interactions.

Jesus has commanded that we love one another, forgiving each other and

living in a gentle and kind-hearted manner toward one another. Even when we have yet to receive our haul after dropping the net of love from our hearts, Jesus advises our return on this investment will be greater than we can imagine.

The acts of brotherly love we commit are the nets Christ uses to gather disciples. Those called to relationships with God find themselves joyfully entangled in the truths, peace, joy, love, and other fruits of the Spirit found in the nets of Christ. Believers are fishermen casting nets into the world's sea of confusion, despair, and unbelief.

Jesus had called these particular fishermen – Simon, Andrew, James and John – to their empty boats and commanded that they cast out from the shore. That is what Jesus does; he fills empty boats and makes them active in His will. The occupied or active fishing boats are not given consideration because Jesus was looking for vessels he could fill with His purpose. Asking the fishermen to cast off is the same message He gives us when He asks us to separate ourselves from ungodly beliefs and actions.

Jesus was in the boat with the fishermen, who would become disciples, speaking as they fished. Once He finished speaking to the crowd that had gathered on land, the fishermen's bounty was hauled. Jesus is in us as we fish for other believers as we share our knowledge of Christ. We, too, are rewarded in the fruitful outcomes of relationships we form through Christ.

We grow spiritually and gain confidence in our profession of faith. We build the house of God which edifies us and ministers to our needs as children of

God. We bless God this way and demonstrate the veracity of our calling, thus being rewarded according to His purpose and will therein.

In Luke's story, it is nighttime, which was considered the best time for net fishing. As Christians, the darkest hours in the lives of those around us are the best times to drop and spread the nets of love God has given us. Just as these are the quietest hours at sea, the lives of those in trouble are quieted by the situation faced. This hour is the best hour to hear and receive the good news of Jesus Christ.

The apostles of Christ would spread the good news as their net and fishing forever changed the world. Our world is changed forever when we use the good news of Jesus Christ as our net.

Using hand nets is the simplest way to fish. You can fish while still on land, but your catch will be small. The bigger, meatier, tastier fish are usually farther out to sea. Ninety-percent of all aquatic life is in the deep. Using hand nets as a believer means you have not challenged yourself beyond the spot where Jesus called you. Instead of casting out to sea, you are trying to enact his will for your life on your terms and in your chosen space and time. This is why some believers are not prospering as they should. The bigger, meatier, tastier blessings are farther out in faith and commitment to God.

Trammel nets are nets that have wood or cork-like bits on the ends. The wood pieces flood in the water and keep the net from sinking to the sea floor. Rocks or clay are used to hold the nets down and keep them from floating away. Trammel nets in the Christian life are kept afloat by our meditation on Jesus' work on the cross. Our belief and acceptance in the atoning sacrifice of Jesus saves us from hitting rock bottom in life. His voluntary crucifixion as an innocent man and God provided a completed act of justice for each of our sins. This truth paved the road for our receipt of God's Spirit, ensuring the word of God would not be dropped by us. The rocks are the truths about Christ and His work in us. The truths inspire us to model Jesus and keep the Word near us.

Drag nets are the Word of God in action. These nets were not weighted down, but dragged through the waters from one location to another. Drag nets represent those not fully receiving the truths of Christ but who are hanging on for miracles and healings. These believers can and will do God's work, when it is convenient or necessary because of some problem or catastrophe. God takes them through situation after situation, dragging them

along instead of them truly walking with Him.

Ghost nets are those which have become disconnected from the boat. These nets are barely visible in dim light. They are found drifting in the open sea or caught on rocky reefs where they entangle fish and other sea creatures. The entangled creatures eventually die and slowly decompose in the ghastly drift.

God tells us that "as the body without the spirit is dead, so faith without works is dead also." If we are not actively manifesting the love of God in the world around us, our faith is dead. A faith that does not shine on and to those nearby is just drifting without connection to God's purpose. This is especially true for those who say they are of God, but do not have the Spirit of God in their hearts or the light of God in their lives. God's light is bright and exposed to all, not hidden away and selective. Any other type of *fishing* only entangles non-believers in the nets of hypocrisy and falsehood, leaving them to drift and decay in their present predicaments and misdirection.

Regardless of the net type, it needs to be cleaned frequently. Cleaning prevents transferring disease from fish to fish. It removes debris and non-fish items trapped in the net. Cleaning the net also provides an opportunity to repair any brittle holes or entanglements that could damage the catch. Likewise, believers must ensure our lives represent the good news we possess. If we are not clean, the messages we transfer in word or deed are unclean.

The debris we pick up from everyday life must be removed each day. We must forgive those who have offended us. We must put past mistakes and failures behind us. We must make sure envy, hate, lust, jealousy, and all the other things floating by are removed from our hearts and actions. Situations, places, people, things that cause us to lose the truths we have gained in the Word must be closed and patched up. Without this thorough cleaning, our fishing would be in vain.

Concern must be given to breaking nets also. In Luke's account, the disciples' net could not hold the huge haul and was breaking. The relationship they had with Jesus at the time was in the infancy stage. They had not walked with Jesus yet and were not prepared to receive all the riches available to them in a walk with Him. Later accounts of fishing with Jesus show they came to be able to handle large catches. We can take on more of God's Word as we walk with Him and strengthen our nets through cleaning and mending.

When proper nets are present, the focus can be placed upon actually catching fish. Fish have a prominent place in biblical illustrations. Fish were the first creatures created in Genesis. They were not taken on the ark with Noah. God used them to redirect a prophet when he had abandoned his mission. *Ichthus*, a Greek word for fish was the earliest Christian symbol. Fishing is used here as a metaphor for lifting up Christ so that he can draw others to Himself.

Fish, like the Word of God, has benefits for those consuming it. Fish is considered brain food – so is biblical scripture. Fish is rich is Omega-3 fatty acids, a natural remedy for a number of health problems – so is God's Word. As fish has been shown to prevent heart disease, the Word has demonstrated its power to change rotten and broken hearts. As fish has been proven to improve poor eyesight, the Word has proven to be a light to the paths of those in dark situations. Fish has remedied depression, and God's Word can lift you out of the miry clay – because it inspires. Eating fish prevents obesity, and in the same vein, the Word of God won't let you get too puffed up about yourself.

When you have the mind of Christ, you share with others. Thus, a second boat appears in Luke's story to share in the catch. The fellowship of believers is the process of sharing the Word of God and our testimonies to its life-changing power. God evinces He is able to abundantly fill us all with overflowing grace, so sharing Him with others is gain for all.

Once Simon realized what Jesus was able to do, he fell at His feet and worshipped Him. Peter was modeling the first step in following Jesus –

admitting he had been unable to succeed at accomplishing his goals outside of Christ, admitting his powerlessness in comparison to the power of God, and finally, admitting his sin in light of Jesus' righteousness.

Simon was an expert fisherman, yet he allowed Jesus to direct him in his area of expertise. We must allow God to direct us in everything, especially those things we believe we know the most about. There is no value in following Christ if you can reach full potential and success at every turn by yourself. The ones who follow Jesus are those who realize – through failure in self and success in Christ – that Jesus is Lord.

Jesus then tells Simon to "fear not." This is recognition that it's frightening to leave a comfort zone for a new life and foreign tasks. The comfort of "fear not" lies in the sure supplication of all needs in our new life and God-given ability. Peter is told that he would be made a "fisher of men." He had truly mastered fishing at sea, and he would learn to master *fishing* on land. In our lives, once we have received enough Word to fill ourselves with a confident and secure faith in God, we have enough to share and fill others as well.

When we follow Jesus, we must do what He did and walk as He walked. The fishing expertise and techniques used by Simon did not work. Jesus' way worked because He is the Way. It was in direct contradiction to what the experts of the time believed to be the right way. Likewise, we have God-given solutions to challenges we face that are contrary to expert suggestions.

LET DOWN YOUR NETS

Walking with Jesus means leaving behind our old ways of doing things and becoming new creatures in Him.

As new creatures, it is no longer about us, but it is all about Him. His plans become our benefits. His purposes become our will. We find our lives in Him and become able to pick them up and lay them down as He wills us. Lives housed in loneliness, fear, and self-contempt find new homes in Christian fellowship, confidence, and Godly exaltation. Lives mired in anger, hate, and depression can be picked up and placed in love, peace, and joy.

In such light, consider who is in your boat with you. Further consider, is it out to sea or sitting idle by the shore? Are there places you should be or want to go in life but you cannot seem to cast out? Is your net weighted down in daily prayer and fellowship with God? Is your net connected to God, or is someone or something else pulling your strings?

No more questions, but one more answer: Jesus.

Let down your net tonight, and receive the great catch God has waiting for you. Jesus is real. He loves you, and He is waiting to bless you.

PRUNING OUR TREES

Chapter Eight

"Every branch in me that beareth not fruit he taketh away: and every branch that beareth fruit, he purgeth it, that it may bring forth more fruit."

John 15:2

The tree is truly one of God's greatest creations. The benefits provided by these creations of providence begin producing the oxygen we need to breathe. They produce fruit and provide fuel for heat and cooking. They reduce soil erosion, promote vegetation and facilitate farming. Trees also provide shade and relief from prolonged exposure to direct sunlight and potentially harmful radiation waves.

Trees offer more contributions but the aforementioned provide enough light to spiritually envision the common threads between trees and Christians. The King James Version of the Holy Bible translates the word tree or trees more than 350 times. Thus, we are urged to consider these references heavily and glean as much wisdom from them as possible.

Perhaps the most light-shedding tree reference was declared by Jesus himself in teaching his disciples that God prunes believers in an effort to increase their productivity. As we understand the purpose of pruning a tree, we are led to a wider understanding of God's purpose in pruning us.

Let us examine this in Spirit, accordingly:

For our purposes, the most fruitful examination involves two types of trees, evergreens and deciduous. Evergreens retain their leaves and remain green throughout the year, whereas deciduous trees change colors and lose their leaves seasonally. Evergreen trees are able to retain their leaves because of a special coating over the leaves and specific genetic makeup that allows them to withstand varying temperatures. Deciduous trees lack the exterior coating and suffer the degrading effects of seasonal climates. These trees' genetic structure directs them to become dormant as light decreases and non-growth periods are established and maintained.

Similarly, evergreen Christians exist and stand in the same fashion as the evergreen trees. Leaves on trees absorb light from the sun and produce the food needed to for the tree to grow. Leaves on Christians are the Godly thoughts, acts and behaviors that allow us to receive and reflect Christ. The Holy Spirit inside of believers allows us to persevere through different seasons, while continuing to walk in a Christian manner with Godly intentions. We coat ourselves with the things Christ would say and do to shield ourselves adequately in unfriendly interactions, situations, and relationships.

Deciduous Christians do not clothe themselves this way. Forgiveness, patience, love, joy, peace, and meekness are not within, and thus, cannot be demonstrated. When the winters of life approach and the hours of sunlight are shortened, these followers begin to change. Less time is spent in prayer,

reading the bible, Christian assembly and meditation. The Godly manners that were temporarily showcased during happier, easier days drop off like the dead leaves on deciduous trees in late fall. This period of dormancy lasts until the spring season of life returns and things start to "warm up." Suddenly, "God is great!" again.

Certainly, much is to be gleaned here. As you look further into Jesus' declaration on pruning, an even more stirring message is given. Self-examination is the starting point in our walk with God. Once our walk begins, maintenance, or pruning is necessary to achieve the abundant life we are promised.

The goal of tree pruning is to produce safe, healthy, and attractive trees. The same goal applies to our spiritual lives. Pruning ourselves with the tools God provides us, produces peaceful, joyful lives that reflect the light of God and demonstrate His goodness to those who believe in Him.

Pruning does not only apply to self, but also to the pruning of those around us. Jesus laid down His life for us as a way of pruning us. His manifestation of God in man trimmed the sin from our lives and repaired our relationship with God. When we lay down our lives for others and demonstrate Jesus in us, we show others how to trim sin from their lives and find relationships with God.

A primary adhesive in the relationship between the ancient Hebrews and God was found in His promise that they would "dwell in the land in safety" if they kept His Commandments. Jesus summed up those Commandments for believers today in His new Commandment that we love one another. Loving one another means saying and doing the things to and for each other that keep us out of harm's way. God explains that where there is no counsel, people fail, but where there is a multitude of counselors, there is safety. If my brother's problem is destroying him, I'm obligated to give him Godly wisdom and assist with resources God has given me for such an occasion. Likewise, if my faults are causing a sister to fail in the purposes God has set

forth for her, I need to trim those behaviors.

Godly decisions are healthy decisions. Certain ways of interacting with others, things we eat or ingest, thought patterns, habits and destructive tendencies result from sin and lead to spiritual and physical death. We must nip these things in the bud and cast them off if we, or those God has commanded us to love, are to survive and grow in Christ. Christian advice and pleasant words are "sweet to the soul, and health to the bones" as described in Proverbs, where God also advises that His wisdom is "health to thy navel, and marrow to thy bones."

In seeking God to assist with correcting our lives and spirits, we realize He is listening as He solves our problems and brightens our outlook on Him, ourselves and the world around us. The book of Psalms agrees in praise when singing "I sought the Lord, and He heard me, and delivered me from all my fears. They looked unto Him, and were lightened: and their faces were not ashamed." Shame creates an ugly look on your situation, your surroundings and your face. God's pruning removes the shame and enlightens us with a newfound confidence in Christ.

However, appropriate pruning techniques must be used. Three common pruning techniques suffice to tie our illustration together: crown Lifting, crown thinning and deadwooding.

Crown lifting involves raising the height of the tree's crown by cutting or trimming low hanging branches. A tree with branches hanging too low can block pathways or hide important messages such as stop signs and danger alerts. Likewise, Christians that engage is the lower pursuits of life – those outside of God's will – are also likely to miss signs and signals God has given.

PRUNING OUR TREES

Crown thinning is the trimming of overgrown exterior foliage. It promotes interior health and growth. While some trees may look beautiful on the exterior, the interior crown may reveal an infestation of pests and disease.

This happens because the overgrowth of exterior branches and leaves will not allow sunlight, oxygen and pesticides to reach the inner crown. The same process can occur with believers who focus solely on maintaining an outwardly Christian appearance while ignoring the application of godly wisdom and principles to their hearts and minds.

Deadwooding promotes safety and is necessary because trees branches die off. The reasons for branches dying are as various as the reasons believers have dead areas in their walk with God. Sometimes leaves aren't getting enough light to make enough food for a healthy tree. Sometimes believers who don't read the Word of God or assemble in fellowship for teaching and exhortation, suffer from the same dying effects: parts of their lives are dead, hanging, and just waiting to fall off. Normally, it takes a while for a dead tree branch to fall off, but the process is sped up in high winds and storms. As a Christian, you can go on living spiritually dead without issue, never realizing how bad off you are until a storm comes and makes it clear.

Some deadwooding situations are more urgent than others. Dead branches overhanging a house, public road, or walking path present more of a hazard than dead branches on a tree in a remote area. It is with this wisdom that deadwooding should be applied. Things that one finds themselves in authority over whether it be children, fellow believers, employees, or any other neighbor should be thoroughly examined for pruning consideration. Godly love and affections should reign and nothing should be done with malice or contempt. If such dead behaviors are found within a believer's tree they should be trimmed and cut out accordingly. Examine your branches and the fruit you produce, and do some pruning in Christ!

SHEEP IN THE MIDST OF WOLVES

Chapter Nine

"As a shepherd seeketh out his flock in the day that he is among his sheep that are scattered; so will I seek out my sheep, and will deliver them out of all places where they have been scattered in the cloudy and dark day. ...I will seek that which was lost, and bring again that which was driven away, and will bind up that which was broken, and will strengthen that which was sick..." Ezekiel 34:12,16

God's tender heart toward His children is often illustrated in His Word as a good shepherd's love for the sheep he tends. The amazingly similar behaviors of believers and sheep provide excellent opportunities for spiritual awakening and direction. Jesus modeled the good Shepherd in His ministry and we, indeed, are modeling sheep in our following Him as our shepherd. By demonstrating God's love in such fashion, Jesus has shown us the mind and heart of God in action. Understanding the illustration of the sheep, the Shepherd and wolves – let us certainly not forget them - leads us to an expanded understanding of God and ourselves.

First to be understood is that sheep are prey animals. When faced with danger, their first instinct is to flee not fight. Their non-aggressive behavior, diet, limited defensive capabilities and mental capacity place them low on the natural food chain, making them food sources for other predatory animals. Likewise, Christians are prey – or pray – animals. We, too, have non-aggressive behaviors. We seek reconciliation and forgiveness in situations that appear to justify retribution and scorn. We look for love, friendship, or peace from those who persecute and hate us.

Our spiritual diet is the Word of God, while those who do not believe in Christ fill themselves with various ideals, theologies, philosophies, and such that are in direct contrast with our beliefs and desired activities. Perpetual prayer becomes a way of life, and God's command to walk in love lives at the forefront of praying minds.

Jesus taught His disciples to turn the other cheek when struck. He taught them to give thieves their coats even when only asked for their shirts. In saying this, He was teaching them to put love before everything, even themselves. People are not are our enemies, sin is our enemy. Sin is evil rulers, evil systems, evil ideals, and other evil spiritual forces beyond our present understanding. God has commanded us to resist these evils by following the direction of His Word. He has told us that the battle against these forces is His. Our direction is to have love for one another.

The love we have for one another mimics the herd behavior we see in sheep. Sheep are gregarious, meaning they tend to stay together in groups while grazing. Sheep instinctively know that banding together keeps them safe from predators seeking strays or those on the edge of the flock. The sheep flee when predators are near, each attempting to get to the center of the group to avoid outer fringes nearest the predator. When the danger is over, the sheep regroup and look at the predator.

In the infancy of the Christian church "all that believed were together, and had all things common." When we assemble ourselves as believers each week, we gain the advantages provided by worshipping our Shepherd together. Banding together in Christian fellowship allows us to share common problems and trade proven solutions found in God's Word. We strengthen each other with real-life testimonies to the power and truth found in scriptures. We show and give each other spiritual and physical love not demonstrated in our everyday environments. A safe and comfortable place in space and time is provided for a celebration of who God is and what He has done in our lives. Each following week, when the dangers of the world have been overcome through Christ, we regroup to graze on God's Word and look back at how God has brought us through.

As we digest Scripture, we mimic the sheep's digestive system. Sheep stomachs have four parts. Each part allows for some digestion and processing of the food until the fourth part completes the final breakdown of nutrients. These four parts correlate with the work of the Father, Son, Holy Ghost and our responding faith. Christians receive and live the Word of God by the Father, Son and Holy Ghost. God expressed Himself through His Word, Jesus. Jesus lives in us through the Spirit. The Spirit confirms in us that we are the children of God and reminds us of His commands. When we give our lives to Christ and He lives in us, we are able to understand God's purpose for our lives and have the power to live according to His will.

However, like sheep we are easily distracted. Because they have such sharp

senses, sheep are always being led to look away, or back or toward some sound or movement. Their keen sense of hearing keeps them turning their ears toward every sound. Their eyes are placed so that they can see behind themselves with a slight turn of the head to either side. This constant looking forward and backward is what keeps them from walking a straight line. The head twist is followed by a rear-end twist to move out of the line of vision. Thus, they create crooked trails.

God has opened the eyes of believers to the ways of the world and His eternal truths. Seeing the opportunity of salvation being handed so openly to those who will accept it, Satan seeks to distract the Christians with anything that will break their focus on God. While reading this book, you may have had multiple distractions in thought, sight and sound that have attempted to divert your focus from these words. Satan knows that if he can keep you turning your head to the right and left you'll go off-track. He wants you to keep looking behind at past mistakes and lost opportunities so that you will not see or reach the promises God has in front of you.

It's truly an uphill battle, which is a good thing. Sheep tend to run uphill and into the wind when stressed. As believers we should also rise when faced with obstacles and difficulties in life. A tough day at work or home calls for prayer, Godly meditation, Christian fellowship for edification and wise counsel. However, often, even believers run downhill to arguing, depression, and destructive behaviors and activities when things are not going as we plan or hope.

The wind and Spirit of God are often used interchangeably in Scripture. When we are faced with trials and tribulations, we should be running into the Spirit of God, not away from it. Our attitude in time of trouble and distress should be hope (not despair), love (not hate), truth (not lying), and prayer (not sedatives or narcotics). Search God's Word for wisdom and understanding. Seek other believers who have gone through similar situations and now understand how to overcome them. Let the Spirit of God guide you though. Use the strong instinct in sheep to follow the sheep in front of them. Like lambs at birth, instinctively follow the leaders of the flock as they flee predators until you are mature enough in Christ to discern good and evil for yourself.

SHEEP IN THE MIDST OF WOLVES

However, be careful in allowing others to lead you spiritually. Be sure they are true believers and followers of Jesus Christ. Jesus warned his disciples to "beware of false prophets, which come to you in sheep's clothing, but inwardly they are ravening wolves."

Wolves can kill healthy sheep, but naturally, they seek the weak, crippled, young, old and sick animals. Satan, as the father of lies, is our wolf. He seeks weak believers who are not really following the commands of God or seeking His will. Satan wants the Christians living life on the fringes of Christianity. In their minds, they maintain a regular fellowship with other believers through occasional attendance of formal assembly. In reality, they only run with the herd when predators are attacking. Church attendance occurs when problems or obstacles arise. However, these are the sheep the wolf seeks. Their life on the edge of faith makes them the most vulnerable targets because they are so far from the life saving truths found in the Shepherd at the center of the herd.

The lameness of these believers makes it a struggle to flee Satan. Blind to the truth of God, they become easy prey as they trip over obstacles, such as lack of patience and forgiveness, envy, hate, jealousy, and apathy. Satan has diseased their minds with desire for ungodly possessions and situations and circumstances. In seeking to obtain these things, they wander from the safety of the Shepherd to the jaws of the wolf.

A wolf's main threat is loss of habitat. When wolves run out of space to live and roam, they die out. God does not want us to give any place in our lives to Satan. Followers of Christ should constantly search all areas of life for Satan's habitat and simply crowd him out with Godly direction. If Satan has found a place in our home, we should increase family church attendance, home bible study, family prayer and general family fellowship. If Satan has a

place in our professions, we should seek scriptural direction on working and how to maintain successful relationships and a good reputation. Wherever evil roams freely in our lives, we should limit its freedom and space until it dies out of our character and actions.

Understand that it may take time, but you can resist the temptation as God leads you into the way of escape He has promised. Wolves can trot 10-15 miles per hour almost indefinitely, so trying to outrun your problems will go on forever. Standing on God's Word will cause wolves to flee because the Word of God will limit the room Satan has to work his evil devices upon your life.

Satan works even harder to get you to go astray as you learn to look for him and these devices. The color of a wolf's pelt can be anywhere from white to black. Likewise, Satan shows up in all colors, shapes and sizes. The brightest light can be hiding the darkest character. Some believers who appear as sheep are actually unbelieving wolves seeking to ravage the character and spirit of true believers for profit and vanity.

Keeping an eye on the Good Shepherd, following His movements and staying in the center of the herd are the keys to an abundant spiritual life. As you get closer to an object, you sense it better, you hear it better, you see it better, and eventually, you can even touch and feel it. The same effect occurs when you follow Jesus as a lamb follows its shepherd. See Jesus as your Shepherd and someone you are willing to follow for all your needs.

FOCUS ON LIGHT

Chapter Ten

"Then Jesus said unto them, Yet a little while is the light with you. Walk while ye have the light, lest darkness come upon you: for he that walketh in darkness knoweth not whither he goeth."

John 12:35

Losing focus is easy to do if you're surrounded by distractions. God knows this and has created us in a fashion that allows us to clearly see only those things upon which we are focusing. This way, anything outside of our focus is blurry and not clearly discernible. The only way to bring things outside of focus to focus is to turn toward them.

The turn is necessary because God has designed us to be facing the things upon which we focus. Our ears are built to best capture sounds that are directly in front of us. The ear protrudes from the head, shaped as a half-cup shape to catch the sound as it passes us. The rings within are designed to carry the sound waves into the ear holes and the hearing process continues on from there. In similar fashion, only those looking to God for direction will hear and understand His plans. Those looking to other things or people for direction will hear and understand those plans clearly, but God's plans will sound dull and shallow as physical sounds are perceived by us when they are made behind us. Imagine the clearer voice. Is it the one in front of you or the one behind you?

In front of you, of course. This is why we must face God with everything we have, including our problems, sins, worries, hopes, dreams, and desires. When we face God with these things, we gain the most clarity in examining them. Then we are able to fully utilize our senses and God-given abilities because we are using them in optimal fashion.

In our physical bodies, we sense the world through five classical senses: hear, see, smell, taste and touch. With the exception of touch, these senses are exclusive to the head, which signals the lead role of the head on our bodies. In our spiritual bodies, Jesus is our head. He is our senses, and coming to Jesus is akin to coming to your senses.

Jesus is the light of the world, and in that light, is life. Light in the physical world is emitted from the sun. It provides energy and facilitates our sense of sight. In the spiritual world, Jesus provides the energized animated state of being we know as life through His will. When we focus on Jesus and operate according to His character and commands, we sense the world around us in the same manner God intended it to operate. We also are able to better align our thoughts and actions with His design. We see things clearly, and thus, we are able to avoid obstacles otherwise unseen and can direct our energies to godly pursuits. This pleases God and creates a more abundant life, but you have to focus on Jesus to achieve it.

Remember, Jesus is the light. Knowing this, consider how we see things in our physical environment. Sight begins when light particles called photons enter our eyes through the pupils. The photons travel to the back of the eye where they are focused on a small patch of cells call the retina. The retina is made up of two types of cells – rods and cones. Cones are in the center of the eye and detect color. They function best in bright light; this is where the eye gives its sharpest detail because it is where the most light is gathered. Rods are on the peripheral edges and function best in low light; rods are colorblind.

Unbelievers also are colorblind. They are constantly in despair and short on hope because they cannot see all of the promises God has made to those who believe Him. Just as a colorful room turns to multiple shades of gray once the room is darkened, the lives of unbelievers turn dark and dreary at every chance to worry and doubt. Even when the rain in life stops, they refuse to look up because there is no bow in the sky for them. Most things are dull and rarely is anything bright, cheerful or exciting reflected by their surroundings.

Having such a sorrowful existence leads to self-pity and spiritual self-exile. Unbelievers find the most satisfaction outside of God's word, numbing themselves in self-deception, failure and destructive planning. Not having light and being uncertain of which path is clear and profitable, they stumble through life as best they can, reacting to one mistake by compounding it with another.

There are about 125 million rods and 6 million cones in the retina. In our world, the ratio appears comparable. Most people enjoy living and walking in darkness. Not only are most not seeking God's light, they are actively avoiding it. Hence, the believer's most important task is to shine the light of God wherever they go to make it clear to others on what they, too, should be focusing.

Believers are cones. Believers live in the light of God by accepting and acting upon His Word. They have been taught the promises of God and have searched the scriptures in study and meditation to ensure the veracity of their lessons. When things in life are dark and gloomy, Christians think and act with brightened and hopeful spirits. Instead of moving away from God and establishing other hopes, they move toward God and ensure they are centered in His Word.

Notice your own vision as you read these words. They are so clear and crisp because you are focused on them. Without turning, look at the things in your peripheral vision. You are able to make them out but you cannot see them in detail. Likewise, when you were looking with your peripheral vision, you lost focus on these words and temporarily abandoned this reading.

Distractions in our focus on God work the same way. God's plan is crystal clear at times of focus in our lives, but being human and imperfect, we sometimes lose that focus. People, places, seasons, and events in our lives can cause us to temporarily lose focus of God's goodness and His plans as we try to make sense of the peripheral challenges.

Keeping our eye on the light is the door to staying focused. Walking in the light is key to keeping our eye on it. The steps of walking in the light consist of the actions when we love others with the love of God. Each good word or deed performed in love by God through us is a step in our walk with God. This is our walk in the Light.

In this fashion, we also know when we are not focused on God and are outside of His will. When we stumble over lies, envy, and deceit, we know we are walking in darkness and looking at life through our cones. When lack of faith keeps us from believing that God will answer our prayers, we should understand and know that we have turned away from the Truth. When we feel undeserving of God's mercy and grace, we should know to search out and turn back toward the light.

Turning back toward the light is deepening our commitment to learning, believing, and trusting in God. Church assembly, Christian fellowship, acts of love and kindness, Bible study, meditation, and prayer are head turners. These things can get your focus back in the right direction, toward the Light of the world.

Jesus is the light of the world because He connects us with the mind of God. The retina sends signals to our brain for interpretation of the light. The signals are sent to the brain by the optic nerve. The brain interprets the light and directs the mind and body on how to best respond to the light.

When we look at things through the mind of Christ, we rely on God's Word to interpret our situations and provide us with our wise and profitable responses. Jesus is the optic nerve connecting us to God's wisdom. It is through Christ that we are able to do all things because in Him we find the wisdom that created all things.

If things are fuzzy and somewhat blurry from your point of view, turn to the light and focus. God deemed whosoever would come to Him in sincere belief of the good news of Jesus Christ would avoid an unfruitful life in this world and be saved from eternal damnation in the next. The good news is that Jesus came as light into the world so that whosoever will believe in Him would not abide in darkness. You are that beloved *whosoever*. Walk in the light. Focus on Jesus.

AMEN.

I LOVE YOU.

GOD BLESS AND KEEP YOU.

21438523R00043

Made in the USA
Middletown, DE
30 June 2015